AFFIRMATIONS OF A
GODLY SPENDER

Daily affirmations to keep God at the centre of your finances.

RIVERLANE PUBLISHING

1ST EDITION

Disclaimer

This book is intended for informational purposes only and does not constitute financial advice. Please consult a licensed professional for guidance tailored to your personal circumstances. Neither the author, publisher, nor editor will be held responsible for any damages or losses—whether resulting from negligence or any other cause—that occur from using or relying on the information provided in this book.

About the *Affirmations* series

The bible-based *Affirmations* series hope to help Christians make decisions in every area of their lives guided by the word of God. Readers can navigate the complexities of life and take simple, daily steps towards their goals.

Affirmations of a Godly Spender is part of the *Affirmations* series with a focus on money management–spending, saving, investing, giving. This edition was compiled and edited by Keji Adebeshin.

The Bible verses in this book are based on the World English Bible British (WEBBE) version.

Giving back

10% of all book sales will be invested in the Riverlane Scholarship Fund to support the education of underprivileged children around the world.

EDITOR'S PREFACE

"Your word is a lamp to my feet, and a light for my path."
Psalm 119:105

God's Word is ever so important in our walk through life. It's the only book in history that explicitly provides a roadmap on how we ought to live *every* aspect of our lives. One of such aspects is financial management.

Money is a powerful tool—it builds as much as it destroys. But as God's children, we're called to be good stewards of money (Matthew 25:14–30) We're called to use our funds responsibly—manage it well, be generous with it, and invest it wisely. Above all, we are to stay solid in our faith and fix our eyes on eternal treasures.

And so, no matter where you are on your journey towards financial peace, the mission of this book is to help you abide in the sweet spot where faith and money intersect.

This daily guide contains 100 verses with practical tips to help you make sound financial decisions. Each day, you'll reflect on a Bible verse, affirm your faith, and take practical action steps. You can also record your progress on the back.

By reflecting on the Word daily, you'll become more intentional of how you think about money—and ultimately how you use it too. Your daily affirmations will ensure your thoughts translate to positive behaviours as you go about your day. Because after all, our thoughts shape our actions (Proverbs 4:23; Matthew 15:18).

DAY 1

GOD'S GOT YOUR BACK

"MY GOD WILL SUPPLY EVERY NEED OF YOURS ACCORDING TO HIS RICHES IN GLORY IN CHRIST JESUS."

PHILLIPIANS 4:19

AFFIRMATION

God's bank never runs out, and He's got me covered. Today, I'm trusting God to cover my needs while I focus on being a blessing to others.

ACTION

Be bold today: Cover someone's coffee, give to a cause that inspires you, or offer help to someone in need. When you give, you're making room for God's blessings to flow back to you.

DAY 2

THE MEASURE OF TRUE WEALTH

"DO NOT LAY UP TREASURES FOR YOURSELVES ON THE EARTH, WHERE MOTH AND RUST CONSUME, AND WHERE THIEVES BREAK THROUGH AND STEAL; BUT LAY UP FOR YOURSELVES TREASURES IN HEAVEN, WHERE NEITHER MOTH NOR RUST CONSUMES, AND WHERE THIEVES DO NOT BREAK THROUGH AND STEAL."

MATTHEW 6:19-20

AFFIRMATION

My money is a tool, and my true wealth is measured in the lives I impact with it. Today, I'll use my money and/or resources to reflect God's heart.

ACTION

Think of one person who could use encouragement today. Send them a message to uplift them. Your act of kindness builds treasure in heaven.

DAY 3

RESEARCH BEFORE YOU RISK

"IT IS NOT GOOD TO HAVE ZEAL WITHOUT KNOWLEDGE, NOR BEING HASTY WITH ONE'S FEET AND MISSING THE WAY."

PROVERBS 19:2

AFFIRMATION

I'll take time to do my research before investing my money. With God's guidance, I'll make decisions that are thoughtful, informed, and rewarding.

ACTION

Before you invest in anything—whether it's stocks, business, real estate, charity, or any other new opportunity—set aside time to research thoroughly. Seek advice from trustworthy sources, pray for clarity, and ensure your enthusiasm is backed by knowledge.

3

DAY 4

LET GOD LEAD

"THE LORD IS MY SHEPHERD; I SHALL LACK NOTHING."

PSALM 23:1

AFFIRMATION

Today, I will trust God fully with my finances and rest in the peace of knowing that He has everything under control.

ACTION

Take a minute to pause and reflect on your financial needs. Ask God to guide you in each area and help you to trust Him more in your spending, saving, and giving.

DAY 5

TRUST IN GOD'S TIMING

"FOR EVERYTHING THERE IS A SEASON, AND A TIME FOR EVERY PURPOSE UNDER HEAVEN."

ECCLESIASTES 3:1

AFFIRMATION

I trust in God's perfect timing for my financial goals. Today, I'll focus on doing the right things with patience, knowing that God will bring the increase when the time is right.

ACTION

Identify one financial goal you've been working towards. Trust God with the timing of that goal and let go of any impatience.

DAY 6

WEALTH WITHOUT WORRY

"THE BLESSING OF THE LORD BRINGS
WEALTH, AND HE ADDS NO TROUBLE TO IT."

PROVERBS 10:22

AFFIRMATION

I receive wealth that brings joy, not stress. I trust God to
guide me towards financial opportunities that align with His
peace.

ACTION

Evaluate one area of your finances. Ask yourself, "Am I
pursuing this with integrity and peace?" Adjust if needed to
reflect God's principles.

DAY 7

GIVE AND RECEIVE

"GIVE, AND IT WILL BE GIVEN TO YOU; GOOD
MEASURE, PRESSED DOWN, SHAKEN
TOGETHER, RUNNING OVER, WILL BE
POURED INTO YOUR LAP. FOR WITH THE
MEASURE YOU USE, IT WILL BE MEASURED
BACK TO YOU."

LUKE 6:38

AFFIRMATION

By giving others my time or resources, I will be blessed in
ways I can't even imagine.

ACTION

Look for an opportunity to give today, whether it's
financially or through time and help. Trust that God will
honour your heart and multiply your generosity.

DAY 8

FOCUS ON WHAT MATTERS

"FOR WHERE YOUR TREASURE IS, THERE YOUR HEART WILL BE ALSO."

MATTHEW 6:21

AFFIRMATION

Above all, I prioritise and treasure serving God, knowing that it holds more value than riches.

ACTION

Reflect on how much time you spend in your walk with God versus financial planning. Today, choose to spend extra time in prayer, worship, reading the Bible, giving, or helping someone out.

DAY 9

CONTENTMENT OVER COMPARISON

"BUT GODLINESS WITH CONTENTMENT IS GREAT GAIN. FOR WE BROUGHT NOTHING INTO THE WORLD, AND IT IS CERTAIN WE CAN CARRY NOTHING OUT."

1 TIMOTHY 6:6-7

AFFIRMATION

I choose to be content and not compare myself with others. Comparison will not steal my joy.

ACTION

Today, make a conscious decision to shake off envy when you see someone in a position you strive to be in. Instead, replace your feelings of lack with gratitude to God for what you have.

DAY 10

PRORITISE AND PLAN

"PREPARE YOUR WORK WITHOUT, AND MAKE IT FIT FOR YOURSELF IN THE FIELD; AND AFTERWARD BUILD YOUR HOUSE."

PROVERBS 24:27

AFFIRMATION

I am intentional with my financial goals. With careful planning, I see myself reaching them with success.

ACTION

Set aside time to review, prioritise and refine your goals. Whether it's paying off debt, investing, starting a business, creating a budget, or preparing for retirement, make sure you have a clear strategy. If not, take the first step today in outlining how to achieve your goal/s.

DAY 11

FIRST FRUITS OF FINANCES

"HONOUR THE LORD WITH YOUR SUBSTANCE, WITH THE FIRSTFRUITS OF ALL YOUR INCREASE: SO YOUR BARNS WILL BE FILLED WITH PLENTY, AND YOUR VATS WILL OVERFLOW WITH NEW WINE."

PROVERBS 3:9-10

AFFIRMATION

I choose to honour God by giving my best, and I trust Him to bless the rest.

ACTION

Review your income and set aside a portion to give back to God–through your church, a ministry, charity, or someone in need.

DAY 12

CONFUSED? PRAY.

"COMMIT YOUR WORKS TO THE LORD, AND
YOUR PLANS WILL BE ESTABLISHED."

PROVERBS 16:3

AFFIRMATION

Today, I choose clarity over confusion.

ACTION

Take a mental account of a financial decision you need to
make. Evaluate your options, then ask God to point you in
the right direction.

DAY 13

KNOW YOUR WORTH

"HE SAID TO THEM, 'TAKE HEED, AND KEEP YOURSELF FROM ALL COVETOUSNESS; FOR A MAN'S LIFE DOESN'T CONSIST OF THE ABUNDANCE OF THE THINGS WHICH HE POSSESSES.'"

LUKE 12:15

AFFIRMATION

My worth goes beyond what I own. My life is rich in faith, love and purpose, not just material things.

ACTION

Take inventory of your life right now. Reflect on three things you're grateful for that money can't buy.

DAY 14

AVOID SHADY DEALINGS

"A FALSE BALANCE IS ABOMINATION TO THE
LORD, BUT A JUST WEIGHT IS HIS DELIGHT."

PROVERBS 11:1

AFFIRMATION

I walk in integrity in my personal and professional dealings.
I will please God by being honest in my pursuit of wealth.

ACTION

Reflect on any financial dealings where you might be
tempted to cut corners or act dishonestly. Commit to being
fair to get the best outcome.

DAY 15

PAY DOWN DEBT

"THE RICH RULE OVER THE POOR. THE BORROWER IS SERVANT TO THE LENDER."

PROVERBS 22:7

AFFIRMATION

I embrace financial freedom; I refuse to be a slave to debt forever.

ACTION

Are you in debt–particularly debt that holds you back or stresses you out? Create a plan to make extra payments this month, cut back on non-essential expense to put towards it, or increase your income over the next few months to pay it off faster.

DAY 16

SECURE YOUR SAVINGS

"HE IS LIKE A MAN BUILDING A HOUSE, WHO DUG DEEP, AND LAID A FOUNDATION ON THE ROCK. WHEN A FLOOD AROSE, THE STREAM BEAT VEHEMENTLY ON THAT HOUSE, AND COULD NOT SHAKE IT, BECAUSE IT WAS FOUNDED ON THE ROCK."

LUKE 6:48

AFFIRMATION

With God's grace, my financial life will be solid enough to withstand any storm.

ACTION

Can your finances get you through tough times? Have you saved for unexpected expenses? If not, plan to either: create an emergency fund that can sustain you for three to six months, create a budget and maintain it every pay cycle, reach out to an accountant for asset protection strategies.

DAY 17

MONITOR YOUR SPENDING

"HE WHO IS FAITHFUL IN A VERY LITTLE IS FAITHFUL ALSO IN MUCH; AND HE WHO IS UNJUST IN A VERY LITTLE IS UNJUST ALSO IN MUCH."

LUKE 16:10

AFFIRMATION

No matter how small or big my bank account is, I will spend wisely.

ACTION

Today, track one expense you often overlook (e.g., daily coffee, subscriptions, lottery). Analyse it and decide whether it aligns with your financial priorities. Adjust if necessary.

DAY 18

FIND A MENTOR

"WITHOUT COUNSEL, PLANS FAIL; BUT IN A MULTITUDE OF COUNSELLORS, THEY ARE ESTABLISHED."

PROVERBS 15:22

AFFIRMATION

With God's counsel, I attract a network of professionals that will increase my net worth.

ACTION

Think of your money goals, then take stock of your circle. Do you surround yourself with people who can mentor you? If so, reach out to one of them today for advice on a financial goal. If not, make it your mission to attend a networking event this year, watch a TED Talk on a financial topic, take a free course online, or read a book with practical advice.

DAY 19

CURB YOUR OBSSESSION

"FOR THE LOVE OF MONEY IS A ROOT OF ALL KINDS OF EVIL, WHICH SOME HAVING COVETED AFTER HAVE ERRED FROM THE FAITH, AND PIERCED THEMSELVES THROUGH WITH MANY SORROWS."

1 TIMOTHY 6:10

AFFIRMATION

I make money moves with pure intentions. I have a healthy relationship with money. I am content and not greedy.

ACTION

Take a moment to reflect on your current financial pursuits. Are they driven by an uncontrollable desire for wealth, or by the desire for financial peace? Make a conscious effort today to refocus your priorities and eliminate any unhealthy attachment to money.

DAY 20

CHOOSE A MASTER

"NO ONE CAN SERVE TWO MASTERS, FOR
EITHER HE WILL HATE THE ONE AND LOVE
THE OTHER, OR ELSE HE WILL BE LOYAL TO
THE ONE AND DESPISE THE OTHER. YOU
CANNOT SERVE GOD AND MAMMON."

MATTHEW 6:24

AFFIRMATION

I am not controlled by my money. Money is a tool; God is my
master.

ACTION

Think of a time you compromised on what you knew to be
right for the sake of financial gain. Ask God to forgive any
misplaced priorities and help you to always put Him first in
your pursuit of financial peace.

DAY 21

SEIZE THE MOMENT

"LOVE NOT SLEEP, LEST YOU COME TO
POVERTY; OPEN YOUR EYES, AND YOU SHALL
BE SATISFIED WITH BREAD."

PROVERBS 20:13

AFFIRMATION

I break free from procrastination and actively seize
opportunities to improve my finances.

ACTION

Is there something you've been putting off? Whether it's
paying off debt, applying for a job, organising receipts, filing
taxes, or exploring an investment opportunity–take one
small action today to move forward.

DAY 22

BUILD SUSTAINABLY

"AN INHERITANCE QUICKLY GOTTEN AT THE BEGINNING WILL NOT BE BLESSED IN THE END."

PROVERBS 20:21

AFFIRMATION

I embrace steady financial progress and resist the temptation of quick, unsustainable rewards.

ACTION

Are you tempted by a get-rich-quick scheme without fully understanding its risks? Reflect on how it aligns with your long-term goals and values. Commit to focusing on consistent, sustainable growth instead.

DAY 23

SET BOUNDARIES

"DON'T BE ONE OF THOSE WHO STRIKE HANDS, OF THOSE WHO ARE SURETIES FOR DEBTS. IF YOU DON'T HAVE ENOUGH TO PAY, WHY SHOULD HE TAKE AWAY YOUR BED FROM UNDER YOU?"

PROVERBS 22:26-27

AFFIRMATION

I honour my financial boundaries and avoid risky commitments that could harm my peace.

ACTION

Make it a rule to never co-sign loans or guarantee debts unless you are fully prepared to take on the responsibility. If you do, ensure you understand the legal and financial implications before moving forward.

DAY 24

WORK AS WORSHIP

"WHATEVER YOU DO, WORK HEARTILY, AS FOR THE LORD AND NOT FOR MEN."

COLOSSIANS 3:23

AFFIRMATION

I produce excellent work even in the face of opposition. I refuse to allow difficult bosses or co-workers to affect my output.

ACTION

If you're frustrated with a difficult coworker or boss, pause, take a deep breath, reset, and remind yourself that your work is ultimately for God.

DAY 25

DIVERSIFY YOUR INCOME

"GIVE A PORTION TO SEVEN, YES, EVEN TO EIGHT; FOR YOU DON'T KNOW WHAT EVIL WILL BE UPON THE EARTH."

ECCLESIASTES 11:2

AFFIRMATION

I welcome multiple streams of income; I attract the resources to build them.

ACTION

If you've already started investing, take time today to review your portfolio and ensure it's diversified. If you haven't, pick an investment vehicle—index funds, real estate, bonds, commodities, peer-to-peer lending, business—and dedicate 30 minutes to learning about its potential benefits.

DAY 26

BOOST YOUR SAVINGS

"THERE IS TREASURE TO BE DESIRED AND OIL IN THE DWELLING OF THE WISE; BUT A FOOLISH MAN SPENDS IT UP."

PROVERBS 21:20

AFFIRMATION

I am a savvy saver. Every amount I save brings me closer to my goals.

ACTION

Try a 'no-spend day' or even a 'no-spend week', and deposit the money saved into your savings account. For added motivation, hide that account from your main banking view so you aren't tempted to dip into it.

DAY 27

MAINTAIN A RAINY-DAY FUND

"GO TO THE ANT, YOU SLUGGARD. CONSIDER HER WAYS, AND BE WISE: WHICH HAVING NO CHIEF, OFFICER, OR RULER, PROVIDES HER BREAD IN THE SUMMER, AND GATHERS HER FOOD IN THE HARVEST."

PROVERBS 6:6-8

AFFIRMATION

I am prepared and protected against unexpected expenses.

ACTION

How's your emergency fund looking? Take time today to review your emergency fund balance and remind yourself why it's important to maintain it. Commit to making sure it's only used for true emergencies.

DAY 28

WALK THE TALK

"IN ALL LABOR THERE IS PROFIT, BUT THE
TALK OF THE LIPS LEADS ONLY TO POVERTY."

PROVERBS 14:23

AFFIRMATION

I am a doer, not a dreamer. I put my words into action to
create the future I desire.

ACTION

Stop planning and start doing—take one small action today
that will bring you closer to your dreams.

DAY 29

KNOW YOUR BUYING POWER

"FOR WHICH OF YOU, DESIRING TO BUILD A
TOWER, DOESN'T FIRST SIT DOWN AND
COUNT THE COST, TO SEE IF HE HAS ENOUGH
TO COMPLETE IT?"

LUKE 14:28

AFFIRMATION

I will invest in the right property and make sure I'm
financially prepared to do so.

ACTION

Before buying a home or investment property, take a close
look at your finances. Ensure you have enough money to
cover the full cost of buying, fixing it up, and maintaining
the property over time.

DAY 30

BALANCE YOUR BOOKS

"BE DILIGENT TO KNOW THE STATE OF YOUR FLOCK, AND PAY CAREFUL ATTENTION TO YOUR HERDS: FOR RICHES ARE NOT FOREVER, NOR DOES THE CROWN ENDURE TO ALL GENERATIONS."

PROVERBS 27:23-24

AFFIRMATION

My financial ledger is in check. My financial peace is on track. With God, my future is set.

ACTION

Set aside time this week to create a personal balance sheet and income statement. The balance sheet will track your assets and liabilities, while the income statement compares your income to your expenses. Regularly update these to stay on top of your finances.

DAY 31

BUY LOW, SELL HIGH

"HE WHO GATHERS IN SUMMER IS A WISE
SON; BUT HE WHO SLEEPS IN HARVEST IS A
SON WHO CAUSES SHAME."

PROVERBS 10:5

AFFIRMATION

I receive God's wisdom to make financial moves at the right
time, when to act and when to wait.

ACTION

Identify areas where you need to wait for the right time to
buy or sell. Create a strategy for when to make your move
and ask for God's leading to do so at the right time.

DAY 32

TRUST THE PROCESS

"CAST YOUR BREAD UPON THE WATERS; FOR
YOU WILL FIND IT AFTER MANY DAYS."

ECCLESIASTES 11:1

AFFIRMATION

I invest my time and resources with boldness, trusting that
my investments will yield great results.

ACTION

Is there a money move that feels a bit scary–perhaps it's
asking for a raise, starting a charity, or making a high-ticket
purchase? Combine your research with faith and seal your
decision with prayer.

DAY 33

SPREAD GOOD VIBES

"THERE IS THAT SCATTERS, AND YET INCREASES; AND THERE IS THAT WITHHOLDS MORE THAN IS MEET, BUT TENDS TO POVERTY."

PROVERBS 11:24

AFFIRMATION

I spread good vibes today, and I receive good vibes in return.

ACTION

Today, do something kind to brighten someone's day—whether it's a compliment, a gift, a generous tip, or an act of service.

DAY 34

FEND FOR YOUR FAMILY

"BUT IF ANY PROVIDES NOT FOR HIS OWN, AND ESPECIALLY FOR THOSE OF HIS OWN HOUSE, HE HAS DENIED THE FAITH, AND IS WORSE THAN AN INFIDEL."

1 TIMOTHY 5:8

AFFIRMATION

I prioritise my loved ones' well-being and watch them thrive in God's goodness. I am a source of blessing in every interaction with them.

ACTION

Do you have dependents? Whether it's a spouse, children, parent, or extended family, spend some quality time with them today and remind them how much they mean to you. Being a provider is about more than just money—it's about love and support.

DAY 35

PAY ON TIME

"YOU SHALL NOT DEFACE THE EDGE OF YOUR NEIGHBOR'S FIELD BY MOVING HIS LANDMARK; YOU SHALL NOT ROB; YOU SHALL NOT WITHHOLD THE HIRED SERVANT'S WAGES, WHETHER THE PERSON BE A BROTHER OR A STRANGER."

LEVITICUS 19:13

AFFIRMATION

I pay all my fines and fees with integrity and a clear conscience.

ACTION

Did someone help you out or do something for you for a price? Don't keep them waiting—pay them fairly and on time to honour their work.

DAY 36

PAY YOUR TAXES

"HE SAID TO THEM, 'THEREFORE RENDER TO CAESAR THE THINGS THAT ARE CAESAR'S, AND TO GOD THE THINGS THAT ARE GOD'S.'"

LUKE 20:25

AFFIRMATION

Through my taxes, I honour my commitment to my community, country, and God's planet.

ACTION

Taxes may not be fun, but they help build the world we live in. Act today: knock out any overdue bills or taxes and celebrate the fact that you're contributing to your community's future.

DAY 37

CONSIDER A SIDE HUSTLE

"IN THE MORNING SOW YOUR SEED, AND IN
THE EVENING WITHHOLD NOT YOUR HAND;
FOR YOU DON'T KNOW WHICH SHALL
PROSPER, WHETHER THIS OR THAT, OR
WHETHER THEY BOTH SHALL BE ALIKE
GOOD."

ECCLESIASTES 11:6

AFFIRMATION

I adopt a growth mindset and I open my mind to new
opportunities that create additional income.

ACTION

Extra income can help you pay down debt faster, invest more,
and save faster for your goals. So today, list your top five
strengths, skills, and abilities. Guess what—there's someone
out willing to pay for any of them.

DAY 38

DON'T OVERWORK YOURSELF

"DO NOT LABOR TO BE RICH. INSTEAD, CEASE
FROM YOUR OWN UNDERSTANDING."

PROVERBS 23:4

AFFIRMATION

Today, I choose to protect my energy and unsubscribe from
hustle culture.

ACTION

Set boundaries for yourself today—whether it's clocking out
on time, taking breaks, or spending quality time with family.
You can't enjoy wealth if you're burned out.

DAY 39

BEWARE OF EASY MONEY

"WEALTH GOTTEN BY VANITY DECREASES, BUT HE WHO GATHERS BY LABOR INCREASES."

PROVERBS 13:11

AFFIRMATION

I am a responsible, money-savvy queen (or king) and I make responsible choices.

ACTION

Beware of people promising double, triple, quadruple returns on your money in a short amount of time. It's often rooted in dishonest business practices. Remember the saying: If it seems too good to be true, it probably is.

DAY 40

PAY IT FORWARD

"AND HE WHO HAD RECEIVED THE FIVE TALENTS CAME AND BROUGHT ANOTHER FIVE TALENTS, SAYING, 'LORD, YOU DELIVERED TO ME FIVE TALENTS. BEHOLD, I HAVE GAINED FIVE MORE TALENTS BESIDE THEM.' HIS LORD SAID TO HIM, 'WELL DONE, GOOD AND FAITHFUL SERVANT. YOU HAVE BEEN FAITHFUL OVER A FEW THINGS. I WILL MAKE YOU RULER OVER MANY THINGS. ENTER INTO THE JOY OF YOUR LORD.'"

MATTHEW 25:20-21

AFFIRMATION

I summon the courage to share God-led money wisdoms with my circle.

ACTION

If you see someone struggling with their finances, share one thing that's helped you manage your money better or solve a problem. Offer to walk them through it or help them set it up.

DAY 41

REMEMBER THE SOURCE

"BUT YOU SHALL REMEMBER THE LORD YOUR GOD, FOR IT IS HE WHO GIVES YOU POWER TO GET WEALTH, THAT HE MAY ESTABLISH HIS COVENANT WHICH HE SWORE TO YOUR FATHERS, AS IT IS THIS DAY."

DEUTERONOMY 8:18

AFFIRMATION

God is my ultimate provider; He is my source of wealth.

ACTION

Take a minute to thank God for the progress you've made so far in your journey towards financial freedom.

DAY 42

KEEP EXPENSES LOW

"WHEN GOODS INCREASE, THEY ARE INCREASED WHO EAT THEM. WHAT GOOD IS THERE TO THE OWNER, EXCEPT TO BEHOLD THEM WITH HIS EYES?"

ECCLESIASTES 5:11

AFFIRMATION

I manage my surplus with wisdom; my income will always exceed my expenses.

ACTION

As your income grows, avoid lifestyle inflation. When you get a pay rise, allocate a portion to savings, debt repayment, fun money, and giving. Adjust the percentages to fit your goals.

DAY 43

REMAIN HUMBLE

"CHARGE THOSE WHO ARE RICH IN THIS PRESENT WORLD, THAT THEY NOT BE HIGHMINDED, NOR HAVE THEIR HOPE SET ON THE UNCERTAINTY OF RICHES, BUT ON GOD, WHO RICHLY GIVES US ALL THINGS TO ENJOY."

1 TIMOTHY 6:17

AFFIRMATION

I'm humble and grounded in my success.

ACTION

Today, focus on being humble in your interactions. Avoid flaunting your achievements. Instead, listen actively and learn from others.

DAY 44

FAITH OVER FORTUNE

"BETTER IS LITTLE, WITH THE FEAR OF THE LORD, THAN GREAT TREASURE AND TROUBLE THEREWITH."

PROVERBS 15:16

AFFIRMATION

Regardless of how much I own or earn, I hold God to the highest regard.

ACTION

As you build your wealth, remember to avoid any sin, temptation or habit that could disrespect God.

DAY 45

DON'T BE ANXIOUS

"THEREFORE DON'T BE ANXIOUS, SAYING, 'WHAT SHALL WE EAT?' OR 'WHAT SHALL WE DRINK?' OR 'WHAT SHALL WE WEAR?' FOR AFTER ALL THESE THINGS THE GENTILES SEEK. FOR YOUR HEAVENLY FATHER KNOWS THAT YOU NEED ALL THESE THINGS. BUT SEEK FIRST GOD'S KINGDOM AND HIS RIGHTEOUSNESS, AND ALL THESE THINGS WILL BE ADDED TO YOU."

MATTHEW 6:31-33

AFFIRMATION

I protect my mental health by releasing all anxiety about my needs.

ACTION

Are you feeling stressed about something? Today, reflect on the last time God came through in your time of need, and trust that He'll do it again.

DAY 46

STAY ROOTED IN CHURCH

"AND ABRAM WAS VERY RICH IN CATTLE, IN SILVER, AND IN GOLD. AND HE WENT ON HIS JOURNEYS FROM THE SOUTH EVEN TO BETHEL, TO THE PLACE WHERE HIS TENT HAD BEEN AT THE BEGINNING, BETWEEN BETHEL AND AI; TO THE PLACE OF THE ALTAR, WHICH HE HAD MADE THERE AT THE FIRST: AND THERE ABRAM CALLED ON THE NAME OF THE LORD."

GENESIS 13:2-4

AFFIRMATION

No matter how much I have, I'll stay planted in God's house.

ACTION

Have you been skipping church lately? If so, commit to attending a service this weekend and stay connected.

DAY 47

MORALS OVER MONEY

"DON'T TRUST IN OPPRESSION, AND DON'T BECOME VAIN IN ROBBERY. IF RICHES INCREASE, DON'T SET YOUR HEART ON THEM."

PSALM 62:10

AFFIRMATION

I hold clean money in my hands and a faithful God in my heart.

ACTION

If you've been prioritising money over morals, hit pause. Pray and shift your focus back to God.

DAY 48

BE FINANCIALLY LITERATE

"THROUGH WISDOM A HOUSE IS BUILT; BY
UNDERSTANDING IT IS ESTABLISHED; AND BY
KNOWLEDGE THE ROOMS ARE FILLED WITH
ALL PRECIOUS AND PLEASANT RICHES."

PROVERBS 24:3-4

AFFIRMATION

My mind is open to continuous learning, knowing that every
lesson brings me closer to financial independence.

ACTION

Take time today to learn something new about money—
whether it's budgeting, investing, or saving. The more you
know, the stronger your financial foundation.

DAY 49

BUY AND SELL FAIRLY

"IF YOU SELL ANYTHING TO YOUR NEIGHBOUR, OR BUY FROM YOUR NEIGHBOUR'S HAND, YOU SHALL NOT OPPRESS ONE ANOTHER."

LEVITICUS 25:14

AFFIRMATION

My money exchanges are ethical and mutually beneficial.

ACTION

Never strike a deal that's detrimental to another person's livelihood.

DAY 50

HEAVEN IS END GAME

"AGAIN I TELL YOU, IT IS EASIER FOR A CAMEL TO GO THROUGH THE EYE OF A NEEDLE, THAN FOR A RICH MAN TO ENTER GOD'S KINGDOM."

MATTHEW 19:24

AFFIRMATION

I position the rest of my life to receive the ultimate prize of heaven.

ACTION

If God were to call you home, would you choose to stay wealthy or go to heaven and leave it all behind? Reflect on this and adjust your priorities.

DAY 51

AVOID OVERINDULGENCE

"HE WHO LOVES PLEASURE WILL BE A POOR MAN. HE WHO LOVES WINE AND OIL WILL NOT BE RICH."

PROVERBS 21:17

AFFIRMATION

As I build my wealth, I release my current and future self from addiction and overconsumption.

ACTION

This week, take a close look at your spending. Identify recurring expenses that offer little value and cut back on them. Commit to moderation in all things.

DAY 52

MAKE GOOD CHOICES

"BETTER IS A LITTLE THAT THE RIGHTEOUS HAVE THAN THE RICHES OF MANY WICKED. FOR THE ARMS OF THE WICKED WILL BE BROKEN, BUT THE LORD UPHOLDETH THE RIGHTEOUS."

PSALM 37:16-17

AFFIRMATION

I stay on the straight and narrow and trust God to keep me secure.

ACTION

As you work on growing your wealth, pause and ask God for wisdom to make choices that keep you on the right path.

DAY 53

GIVE CHEERFULLY

"LET EACH MAN GIVE ACCORDING AS HE HAS PURPOSED IN HIS HEART, NOT GRUDGINGLY, OR OF NECESSITY: FOR GOD LOVES A CHEERFUL GIVER."

2 CORINTHIANS 9:7

AFFIRMATION

My giving is intentional, heartfelt, and pleasing to God.

ACTION

Does a friend, co-worker or loved one have a birthday coming up? Plan a gift from your heart that will make them feel truly celebrated.

DAY 54

LEND WITHOUT INTEREST

"IF YOU LEND MONEY TO ANY OF MY PEOPLE
WITH YOU WHO IS POOR, YOU SHALL NOT BE
TO HIM AS A LENDER; NEITHER SHALL YOU
LAY UPON HIM USURY."

EXODUS 22:25

AFFIRMATION

I am compassionate in my financial dealings with the
vulnerable.

ACTION

If someone struggling financially asks for a loan and you're
able to help, lend without interest to ease their burden.

DAY 55

SOW FOR SUCCESS

"HE WHO TILLS HIS LAND WILL HAVE PLENTY
OF BREAD, BUT HE WHO CHASES VANITY
WILL HAVE POVERTY ENOUGH."

PROVERBS 28:19

AFFIRMATION

Today, I exert my energy on work that brings me reward.

ACTION

What financial goal can you continue to work on today?
Avoid distractions, focus on it, and remember that
consistency leads to progress.

DAY 56

STAY TRUE TO YOURSELF

"FOR WHAT DOES IT PROFIT A MAN TO GAIN THE WHOLE WORLD, AND FORFEIT HIS SOUL?"

MARK 8:36

AFFIRMATION

No matter how much money I make, I'll stay true to who I am in God.

ACTION

Take a moment today to ask yourself: Is what I'm chasing bringing me closer to God, or pulling me away from my morals and values?

DAY 57

THE REWARD OF OBEDIENCE

"PRAISE THE LORD! BLESSED IS THE MAN WHO FEARS THE LORD, WHO DELIGHTS GREATLY IN HIS COMMANDMENTS. HIS OFFSPRING WILL BE MIGHTY IN THE LAND. THE GENERATION OF THE UPRIGHT WILL BE BLESSED. WEALTH AND RICHES ARE IN HIS HOUSE. HIS RIGHTEOUSNESS ENDURES FOREVER."

PSALM 112:3

AFFIRMATION

In my obedience to God, I claim the reward of wealth and build a legacy of abundance.

ACTION

What has God put in your heart lately to do? Today, set aside your pride or fear and gather the courage to do it.

DAY 58

SPEND YOUR SURPLUS WISELY

"WHATEVER SEEMETH GOOD TO YOU AND
TO YOUR BROTHERS TO DO WITH THE REST
OF THE SILVER AND THE GOLD, THAT DO
AFTER THE WILL OF YOUR GOD."

EZRA 7:18

AFFIRMATION

I view my extra resources as opportunities to serve, do good
and please God.

ACTION

Do you have spare change? Give it to the less fortunate today.

DAY 59

DON'T BE GREEDY

"HE WHO IS GREEDY FOR GAIN TROUBLES HIS OWN HOUSEHOLD, BUT HE WHO HATES BRIBES WILL LIVE."

PROVERBS 15:27

AFFIRMATION

Greed is a trap—I refuse to let it destroy my peace, home, or future.

ACTION

Today, take a minute to ask God for the courage to walk away from any money-making opportunity that feels off or shady. Trust that there is a better deal just around the corner.

DAY 60

HELP YOUR KIN

"IF YOUR BROTHER BECOMES POOR, AND HIS
HAND FAILS WITH YOU, THEN YOU SHALL
SUPPORT HIM: HE SHALL LIVE WITH YOU AS A
STRANGER, AND A SOJOURNER. TAKE NO
USURY OF HIM, OR INTEREST; BUT FEAR
YOUR GOD; THAT YOUR BROTHER MAY LIVE
WITH YOU. YOU SHALL NOT LEND HIM YOUR
MONEY AT USURY, NOR LEND HIM YOUR
FOOD FOR INCREASE."

LEVITICUS 25:35-37

AFFIRMATION

I exercise the privilege to help my family without hesitation
and expectations.

ACTION

Reach out to a family member today—whether they need
help or just a check-in—and let them know that you're there
for them.

DAY 61

MAINTAIN PERSPECTIVE

"DO NOT BE AFRAID WHEN A MAN BECOMES RICH, WHEN THE GLORY OF HIS HOUSE IS INCREASED; FOR WHEN HE DIES HE SHALL CARRY NOTHING AWAY. HIS GLORY SHALL NOT DESCEND AFTER HIM."

PSALM 49:16-17

AFFIRMATION

I'm not swayed by the rich, the famous, or the illusions of temporary wealth.

ACTION

When you catch yourself envying the success of others, pause and remind yourself that true wealth is not found in fame or fortune, but in living with purpose.

DAY 62

AVOID BRIBES

"YOU SHALL TAKE NO BRIBE, FOR A BRIBE BLINDS THOSE WHO HAVE SIGHT, AND PERVERTS THE WORDS OF THE RIGHTEOUS."

EXODUS 23:8

AFFIRMATION

Integrity is my currency, and I spend it wisely.

ACTION

No matter how tempting it is, never give or receive bribes that could compromise your values.

DAY 63

PLAN WITH PATIENCE

"THE THOUGHTS OF THE DILIGENT TEND ONLY TO PLENTY; BUT EVERY ONE WHO IS HASTY ONLY TO WANT."

PROVERBS 21:5

AFFIRMATION

My financial success is built on patience, not haste; planning, not speculation.

ACTION

Don't make hasty financial decisions out of fear, excitement, or desperation. Take your time, do your research, and plan it out. That way, you'll increase your chances of success.

DAY 64

DON'T BE DISTRACTED

"BUT THE CARES OF THIS WORLD, AND THE DECEITFULNESS OF RICHES, AND THE LUSTS OF OTHER THINGS ENTERING IN, CHOKE THE WORD, AND IT BECOMES UNFRUITFUL."

MARK 4:19

AFFIRMATION

I prioritise my spiritual growth over vain distractions.

ACTION

Take 30 minutes today to silence your phone, read a chapter from the Bible, and reflect on its message. Pray about it afterwards.

DAY 65

DO GODLY BUSINESS

"A MERCHANT HAS DISHONEST SCALES IN
HIS HAND. HE LOVES TO DEFRAUD. EPHRAIM
SAID, 'SURELY I HAVE BECOME RICH. I HAVE
FOUND WEALTH FOR MYSELF. IN ALL MY
LABOURS THEY WON'T FIND IN ME ANY
INIQUITY THAT IS SIN.'"

HOSEA 12:7-8

AFFIRMATION

My business transactions are grounded in honesty, not
deceit; I credit God as the source of my blessings.

ACTION

Do you have a business or side hustle, or are you planning to
start one? Avoid fraud and treat your customers and
suppliers fairly. Remain humble and acknowledge God as the
reason for your success.

DAY 66

MIND YOUR BUSINESS

"AND THAT YOU STUDY TO BE QUIET, AND TO DO YOUR OWN BUSINESS, AND TO WORK WITH YOUR OWN HANDS, EVEN AS WE COMMANDED YOU; THAT YOU MAY WALK HONESTLY TOWARD THEM THAT ARE WITHOUT, AND THAT YOU MAY HAVE LACK OF NOTHING."

1 THESSALONIANS 4:11-12

AFFIRMATION

I make money moves in silence; I focus on the grind with diligence.

ACTION

This week, exercise discretion and avoid oversharing about your finances.

DAY 67

PROTECT YOUR HEALTH

"DO NOT WEARY YOURSELF TO GAIN WEALTH. CEASE FROM YOUR OWN UNDERSTANDING. WILL YOU SET YOUR EYES ON THAT WHICH IS NOT? FOR RICHES CERTAINLY MAKE THEMSELVES WINGS. THEY FLY AWAY AS AN EAGLE TOWARD HEAVEN."

PROVERBS 23:4-5

AFFIRMATION

I work with discernment, knowing when to pause and rest. I prioritise my health and happiness over the endless pursuit of wealth.

ACTION

When was your last health checkup? Make a list today of steps to prioritise your health—like eating better, exercising, booking that doctor's appointment, or even treating yourself to a staycation or getaway.

67

DAY 68

GIVE TO GOD'S WORK

"BRING THE WHOLE TITHE INTO THE STOREHOUSE, THAT THERE MAY BE FOOD IN MY HOUSE, AND TEST ME NOW IN THIS," SAYS THE LORD OF ARMIES, "IF I WILL NOT OPEN YOU THE WINDOWS OF HEAVEN, AND POUR YOU OUT A BLESSING, THAT THERE SHALL NOT BE ROOM ENOUGH TO RECEIVE IT."

MALACHI 3:10

AFFIRMATION

The more I give to God's work, the more I'm blessed beyond measure.

ACTION

Take a moment to reflect on how you can support God's work–whether through a building project, charity, mission, or directly as a church offering. Trust that in return, God will bless you abundantly.

DAY 69

GIVE TO THE NEEDY

"IF THERE IS A POOR MAN WITH YOU, ONE OF YOUR BROTHERS, IN ANY OF YOUR GATES IN YOUR LAND WHICH THE LORD YOUR GOD GIVES YOU, YOU SHALL NOT HARDEN YOUR HEART, NOR SHUT YOUR HAND FROM YOUR POOR BROTHER."

DEUTERONOMY 15:7

AFFIRMATION

I am a vessel of generosity to those in need. I'm called to comfort, not criticise.

ACTION

If you can, set aside some money from your next pay cheque to donate to a shelter in your city, or a cause that supports those in need.

DAY 70

GIVE WITHOUT EXPECTATIONS

"IF YOU LEND TO THOSE FROM WHOM YOU
HOPE TO RECEIVE, WHAT CREDIT IS THAT TO
YOU? EVEN SINNERS LEND TO SINNERS, TO
RECEIVE BACK AS MUCH."

LUKE 6:34

AFFIRMATION

I give out of the goodness of God with no strings attached.

ACTION

The next time you lend to family or friends, do so without
expecting it back. Give freely, knowing that it's an act of love,
not a transaction.

DAY 71

THE LIMITS OF WEALTH

"RICHES DON'T PROFIT IN THE DAY OF WRATH, BUT RIGHTEOUSNESS DELIVERS FROM DEATH."

PROVERBS 11:4

AFFIRMATION

Money is a tool, not a saviour. I move with honesty and stay glued to God's mercy and divine protection.

ACTION

Today, think about the times when money couldn't fix things, but God came through. Ask Him to help you keep living right and guide you through any challenges ahead.

DAY 72

GOD IS IN CONTROL

"THE LORD MAKES POOR, AND MAKES RICH.
HE BRINGS LOW, HE ALSO LIFTS UP."

1 SAMUEL 2:7

AFFIRMATION

I remain humble in both success and setbacks, knowing that
God is in control.

ACTION

As God oversees every step of your financial journey,
remember to approach your wins and challenges with
humility.

DAY 73

HAVE A BREAK

"THERE IS ONE WHO IS ALONE, WITHOUT COMPANION; HE HAS NEITHER SON NOR BROTHER. YET THERE IS NO END TO ALL HIS LABOURS; NEITHER IS HIS EYE SATISFIED WITH RICHES. 'FOR WHOM THEN DO I LABOUR, AND DEPRIVE MYSELF OF GOOD?' THIS ALSO IS VANITY. YES, IT IS A SORROWFUL TASK."

ECCLESIASTES 4:8

AFFIRMATION

I refuse to chase success at the cost of my mental well-being. As I build wealth with purpose, I also create space for rest, joy, and relationships.

ACTION

This week, set clear boundaries between work and personal time. Plan a day to recharge—whether it's a solo or group outing, movie night, game night, or quality time with loved ones.

DAY 74

CELEBRATE OUTWARDS

"AS THE DAYS WHEN THE JEWS RESTED FROM
THEIR ENEMIES, AND THE MONTH WHICH
WAS TURNED TO THEM FROM SORROW TO
JOY, AND FROM MOURNING INTO A GOOD
DAY; THAT THEY SHOULD MAKE THEM DAYS
OF FEASTING AND JOY, AND OF SENDING
PORTIONS ONE TO ANOTHER, AND GIFTS TO
THE POOR."

ESTHER 9:22

AFFIRMATION

As I experience financial success, I will express gratitude to
God by blessing those around me.

ACTION

Whenever you hit a financial milestone, take time to reward
yourself. But don't forget to also bless someone else–whether
it's a one-time act or an ongoing gesture.

DAY 75

REMEMBER TO GIVE

"HE WHO HAS A GENEROUS EYE WILL BE
BLESSED; FOR HE SHARES HIS BREAD WITH
THE POOR."

PROVERBS 22:9

AFFIRMATION

As I give, I am blessed knowing that blessings always come
back around.

ACTION

Today, find a way to give—whether it's helping someone out,
sharing a meal, or just offering your time.

DAY 76

OWE NOTHING

"OWE NO ONE ANYTHING, EXCEPT TO LOVE ONE ANOTHER; FOR HE WHO LOVES HIS NEIGHBOUR HAS FULFILLED THE LAW."

ROMANS 13:8

AFFIRMATION

Debt is expensive, love is free. I embrace a debt-free life and God-filled love.

ACTION

Do you know your debt-free date? If not, this week, organise your debts into 'current' (must be paid within 12 months), 'intermediate' (1-5 years), or 'long-term' (5+ years). Create a repayment plan for each category and track your progress as you pay them off. Look for ways to speed up your payments to get closer to your debt-free date.

DAY 77

SPEND ON VALUE

"WHY DO YOU SPEND MONEY FOR THAT WHICH IS NOT BREAD? AND YOUR LABOUR FOR THAT WHICH DOES NOT SATISFY? LISTEN DILIGENTLY TO ME, AND EAT THAT WHICH IS GOOD, AND LET YOUR SOUL DELIGHT ITSELF IN FATNESS."

ISAIAH 55:2

AFFIRMATION

I am intentional with my spending; I spend on things that bring me joy and add value to my life.

ACTION

Before you buy something, ask yourself: "What value does this bring me? Is it worth it?"

DAY 78

GIVE AND LET GO

"GIVE TO EVERYONE WHO ASKS YOU, AND OF
HIM WHO TAKES AWAY YOUR GOODS DO NOT
ASK THEM BACK."

LUKE 6:30

AFFIRMATION

I freely give to others without expectations or resentment.

ACTION

Release any desire to chase after what others owe you,
trusting that God will restore any loss.

DAY 79

CONSCIENCE OVER COMPROMISE

"BETTER IS A LITTLE WITH RIGHTEOUSNESS
THAN GREAT REVENUE WITH INJUSTICE."

PROVERBS 16:8

AFFIRMATION

I refuse to compromise my conscience for the sake of wealth.

ACTION

As you level up on your financial journey, be sure to avoid any dishonest earnings that can compromise your relationship with God.

DAY 80

REFRAIN FROM THEFT

"AS THE PARTRIDGE SITS ON EGGS AND HATCHES THEM NOT, SO HE WHO GETS RICHES, AND NOT BY RIGHT, WILL LEAVE THEM IN THE MIDST OF HIS DAYS, AND AT HIS END WILL BE A FOOL."

JEREMIAH 17:11

AFFIRMATION

I earn money the right way, knowing that my honest gains will stick.

ACTION

To make sure your wealth lasts, review your income sources and ensure they come from honest means. Avoid taking credit for what isn't yours.

DAY 81

BE YOURSELF

"BETTER IS HE WHO IS LIGHTLY ESTEEMED, AND HAS A SERVANT, THAN HE WHO HONOURS HIMSELF, AND LACKS BREAD."

PROVERBS 12:9

AFFIRMATION

I prioritise substance over status. I'm focused on my own journey, not others'. I am confident, authentic, and enough.

ACTION

Whenever you feel tempted to 'keep up with the Joneses', remember that your worth comes from God, not from external appearances.

DAY 82

SPEAK WITHOUT ENVY

"LET YOUR CONVERSATION BE WITHOUT COVETOUSNESS; AND BE CONTENT WITH SUCH THINGS AS YOU HAVE: FOR HE HAS SAID, 'I WILL NEVER LEAVE YOU, NOR FORSAKE YOU.'"

HEBREWS 13:5

AFFIRMATION

I speak with faith, contentment, and positivity, focusing on what I have, not what I lack.

ACTION

This week, celebrate the wins of those around you. If comparison creeps in, remember God is ever present—and that's the ultimate blessing.

DAY 83

PUT IN THE WORK

"HE WHO HAS A SLACK HAND BECOMES POOR, BUT THE HAND OF THE DILIGENT BRINGS WEALTH."

PROVERBS 10:4

AFFIRMATION

I honour my time and stay productive, knowing that my hard work will lead to success.

ACTION

Today, pick one task you've been putting off and tackle it with full effort.

DAY 84

CURB YOUR PRIDE

"THUS SAYS THE LORD, 'LET NOT THE WISE MAN GLORY IN HIS WISDOM, NEITHER LET THE MIGHTY MAN GLORY IN HIS MIGHT, LET NOT THE RICH MAN GLORY IN HIS RICHES. BUT LET HIM WHO GLORIES GLORY IN THIS, THAT HE UNDERSTANDS AND KNOWS ME, THAT I AM THE LORD WHO EXERCISES LOVINGKINDNESS, JUSTICE, AND RIGHTEOUSNESS IN THE EARTH; FOR IN THESE THINGS I DELIGHT,' SAYS THE LORD."

JEREMIAH 9:23-24

AFFIRMATION

I choose to brag about God, not money.

ACTION

In your conversations about money, don't boast or act proud. Rather, acknowledge God—the giver of all things.

DAY 85

DON'T EXPLOIT OTHERS

"THEREFORE BECAUSE YOU TRAMPLE ON THE POOR, AND TAKE FROM HIM EXACTIONS OF WHEAT, YOU HAVE BUILT HOUSES OF HEWN STONE, BUT YOU SHALL NOT DWELL IN THEM; YOU HAVE PLANTED PLEASANT VINES, BUT YOU SHALL NOT DRINK WINE FROM THEM."

AMOS 5:11

AFFIRMATION

I will uplift and not exploit to enjoy the fruits of my labour.

ACTION

If you're in a management role or a position of power, remember to treat your people fairly and never take advantage of them financially.

DAY 86

TRUST IN GOD, NOT RICHES

"HE WHO TRUSTS IN HIS RICHES WILL FALL, BUT THE RIGHTEOUS SHALL FLOURISH AS THE GREEN LEAF."

PROVERBS 11:28

AFFIRMATION

Regardless of my net worth, I choose to trust God in all circumstances.

ACTION

Remember, wealth is temporary, but God is eternal. In your financial journey, let God take the lead as you walk by faith with Him.

DAY 87

PREPARE BENEFICIARIES

"FOR THERE IS A MAN WHO HAS LABOURED WITH WISDOM, AND WITH KNOWLEDGE, AND WITH SKILL; AND YET TO A MAN WHO HAS NOT LABOURED IN IT SHALL HE LEAVE IT AS HIS PORTION. THIS ALSO IS VANITY AND A GREAT EVIL."

ECCLESIASTES 2:21

AFFIRMATION

The legacy I build will go to deserving and responsible hands.

ACTION

Today, reflect on where you want your wealth to go in your absence. Whether it's to loved ones, charity, or other causes, make sure they have the knowledge and tools to manage it wisely. If you haven't already, research *estate planning* and create a solid plan.

DAY 88

APPRECIATE EVERY MOMENT

"COME NOW, YOU WHO SAY, 'TODAY OR
TOMORROW WE WILL GO INTO THIS CITY,
AND SPEND A YEAR THERE, AND CARRY ON
BUSINESS, AND MAKE A PROFIT.' YOU DON'T
KNOW WHAT YOUR LIFE WILL BE LIKE
TOMORROW. FOR WHAT IS YOUR LIFE? FOR
YOU ARE A VAPOR THAT APPEARS FOR A
LITTLE TIME, AND THEN VANISHES AWAY."

JAMES 4:13-14

AFFIRMATION

Today, I choose to be present and let go of what's beyond my
control.

ACTION

Set goals, make plans, but don't stress over tomorrow. Trust
God, take it one step at a time, and make the most of today.

DAY 89

INVEST IN OTHERS

"HE WHO HAS PITY ON THE POOR LENDS TO
THE LORD, AND HE WILL PAY HIM AGAIN."

PROVERBS 19:17

AFFIRMATION

Helping others is my divine investment. God's blessings are
my reward.

ACTION

If you know someone struggling, give, share, or support in
any way you can. Trust that God will credit it to you in
blessings.

DAY 90

ENJOY YOUR SUCCESS

"EVERY MAN ALSO TO WHOM GOD HAS
GIVEN RICHES AND WEALTH, AND HAS
GIVEN HIM POWER TO EAT OF IT, AND TO
TAKE HIS PORTION, AND TO REJOICE IN HIS
LABOUR—THIS IS THE GIFT OF GOD."

ECCLESIASTES 5:19

AFFIRMATION

I deserve to splurge and indulge in the things I enjoy with
moderation. I refuse to hoard wealth or be selfish to myself.

ACTION

Today, review your budget and set aside a percentage of your
regular income for 'fun money'. Use this money to treat
yourself to things or experiences that bring you joy, without
guilt.

DAY 91

LAY THE RIGHT FOUNDATION

"WOE TO HIM WHO BUILDS HIS HOUSE BY
UNRIGHTEOUSNESS, AND HIS CHAMBERS BY
WRONG; WHO USES HIS NEIGHBOUR'S
SERVICE WITHOUT WAGES, AND GIVES HIM
NOTHING FOR HIS WORK."

JEREMIAH 22:13

AFFIRMATION

I build my financial freedom on a Godly foundation without
exploitation or extortion.

ACTION

As you build your financial house, remember not to take
advantage of others just to get ahead. Be sure to treat and
reward anyone who helps you in the process fairly.

DAY 92

RETAIN FUTURE GAINS

"THOUGH HE HEAPS UP SILVER AS DUST, AND PREPARES RAIMENT AS THE CLAY; HE MAY PREPARE IT, BUT THE JUST SHALL PUT IT ON, AND THE INNOCENT SHALL DIVIDE THE SILVER."

JOB 27:16-17

AFFIRMATION

As I build wealth with merit, my rewards will not evade me.

ACTION

Today, take a moment to reflect on your 'why'. Remember, to fully accomplish your 'why'–that is, the fruits of your savings and investments, make sure you're earning those gains with a clear conscience.

DAY 93

BALANCE OVER BETRAYAL

"REMOVE FAR FROM ME VANITY AND LIES; GIVE ME NEITHER POVERTY NOR RICHES; FEED ME WITH FOOD CONVENIENT FOR ME: LEST I BE FULL, AND DENY YOU, AND SAY, 'WHO IS THE LORD?' OR LEST I BE POOR, AND STEAL, AND TAKE THE NAME OF MY GOD IN VAIN."

PROVERBS 30:8-9

AFFIRMATION

I refuse to compromise my faith for my impending fortune.

ACTION

As you improve in money management and start seeing results, be humble. Avoid getting caught up in pride or greed that could pull you away from God.

DAY 94

GET OUT WHAT YOU PUT IN

"BUT THIS I SAY: HE WHO SOWS SPARINGLY WILL ALSO REAP SPARINGLY; AND HE WHO SOWS BOUNTIFULLY WILL ALSO REAP BOUNTIFULLY."

2 CORINTHIANS 9:6

AFFIRMATION

I earn according to the measure that I give to others and invest in my future.

ACTION

If you're investing—whether for retirement, education, a home, or other goals, do you know your investing horizon? If not, take the time today to calculate how much you need to achieve your goals. Then, work backwards to determine how much you should invest regularly, and set it in motion.

DAY 95

MONEY ≠ HAPPINESS

"THE SLEEP OF A LABOURING MAN IS SWEET,
WHETHER HE EATS LITTLE OR MUCH; BUT
THE ABUNDANCE OF THE RICH WILL NOT
SUFFER HIM TO SLEEP."

ECCLESIASTES 5:12

AFFIRMATION

I'm on a journey towards financial peace, not stress. I use my money for things and experience that bring comfort, not struggle.

ACTION

Money is a tool, not the goal. As your net worth grows, remember to prioritise rest and well-being.

DAY 96

DRAMA-FREE FORTUNE

"IN THE HOUSE OF THE RIGHTEOUS IS MUCH TREASURE, BUT IN THE REVENUE OF THE WICKED IS TROUBLE."

PROVERBS 15:6

AFFIRMATION

With my integrity intact, I build a household of treasure, not trouble.

ACTION

Today, take a moment to reflect on how your money decisions impact those you care about, particularly dependents. Does it bring them peace? If not, commit to making better choices that benefit them.

DAY 97

THE CURSE OF CORRUPTION

"COME NOW, YOU RICH, WEEP AND HOWL FOR YOUR MISERIES THAT ARE COMING UPON YOU. YOUR RICHES ARE CORRUPTED, AND YOUR GARMENTS ARE MOTH-EATEN. YOUR GOLD AND SILVER ARE CANKERED; AND THE RUST OF THEM SHALL BE A WITNESS AGAINST YOU, AND SHALL EAT YOUR FLESH AS IT WERE FIRE. YOU HAVE HEAPED TREASURE TOGETHER FOR THE LAST DAYS."

JAMES 5:1-3

AFFIRMATION

I reject corrupt money and embrace Godly gains.

ACTION

Check how you're making money today. Ensure you're staying true to God's values to avoid regret later.

DAY 98

LEAVE A LASTING IMPACT

"AS HE CAME FORTH OF HIS MOTHER'S WOMB, NAKED SHALL HE RETURN TO GO AS HE CAME, AND SHALL TAKE NOTHING OF HIS LABOUR, WHICH HE MAY CARRY AWAY IN HIS HAND."

ECCLESIASTES 5:15

AFFIRMATION

Nothing lasts forever but the Word of God, eternity, and the impact I leave behind.

ACTION

As you build your wealth, think about how you can use your resources to create generational impact. Whether it's Climate Change, Children's Welfare, Health, Homelessness, Ministry—whatever it is, create a sustainable goal using the S.M.A.R.T. acronym: Specific, Measurable, Achievable, Realistic, and Time-based. Then, work towards it.

DAY 99

DON'T SWEAT LOSSES

"FOR WE KNOW THAT IF OUR EARTHLY
HOUSE OF THIS TABERNACLE WERE
DISSOLVED, WE HAVE A BUILDING OF GOD, A
HOUSE NOT MADE WITH HANDS, ETERNAL
IN THE HEAVENS."

2 CORINTHIANS 5:1

AFFIRMATION

I am as fearless in losses as I am in wins, knowing that God is
my north star.

ACTION

Financial losses might hurt, but they're not the end of the
story. As you face setbacks, keep your focus on the bigger
picture. Keep investing in your faith and purpose, knowing
that they'll outlast any material loss.

DAY 100

DON'T BE DISCOURAGED

"FOR THEY ALL MADE US AFRAID, SAYING, 'THEIR HANDS SHALL BE WEAKENED FROM THE WORK, THAT IT BE NOT DONE.' NOW THEREFORE, O GOD, STRENGTHEN MY HANDS."

NEHEMIAH 6:9

AFFIRMATION

I am grounded, focused and resilient on my journey to financial peace. With God, I'll reach my goals.

ACTION

Ignore the naysayers—your personal finance journey is just that: personal. Measure your progress against your past self, not others' expectations. Today, ask God for the confidence to stay committed to your plans.

PROGRESS UPDATES

_____

_____

_____

_____

_____

_____

_____

_____

_____

_____

_____

_____

_____

_____

_____

_____

_____

_____

INDEX

A
Anxiety – Days 4, 5, 6, 12, 44, 45, 95, 100
Asset Protection – Days 16, 25, 30, 92

B
Bribery – Day 62
Budgeting – Days 10, 29, 30
Business – Days 3, 14, 49, 65, 91

C
Church – Days 11, 46, 68
Comparison – Days 1, 9, 13, 61, 81, 82

D
Debt – Days 15, 23, 35, 54, 76
Delayed Gratification – Days 5, 22, 32
Diversification – Days 25, 37
Discretion – Day 66

E
Emergency Fund – Days 16, 27

F
Family – Days 34, 60, 87, 96
Financial Literacy – Days 29, 48
Frugality – Days 17, 26, 42, 51

G
Generational Wealth – Days 57, 87
Giving – Days 1, 7, 11, 33, 53, 58, 68, 69, 75, 78, 89, 97
Greed – Days 14, 19, 39, 47, 59, 80
Gratitude – Days 9, 13, 74, 88

H
Health – Days 38, 45, 67, 73, 95
Humility – Days 41, 43, 72, 84, 88, 93

I
Income – Days 25, 37, 42
Integrity – Days 14, 17, 34, 47, 49, 52, 56, 57, 62, 65, 71, 79, 80, 85, 91, 92, 96
Investing – Days 3, 25, 31, 32, 40, 92, 94

L

Lending – Days 54, 60, 70, 78

Legacy – Days 57, 87, 98

Lifestyle Inflation – Days 42, 51

M

Mentorship – Day 18

Moderation – Days 38, 42, 51, 93

O

Opportunities – Days 21, 25, 31, 37, 40

Overworking – Days 38, 67, 73

P

Patience – Days 5, 22, 32, 63

Planning – Days 3, 10, 16, 18, 63

Prayer – Days 12, 100

Prioritisation – Days 8, 10, 20, 50, 64

Procrastination – Days 21, 28

Property – Day 29

R

Relationships – Days 34, 40, 49, 60, 73

Risk – Days 3, 16, 22, 23, 29, 39, 88, 94

S

Saving – Days 16, 26, 27

Spending – Days 17, 42, 49, 51, 58, 77, 90

Spiritual Wealth – Days 2, 8, 44, 45, 50, 99

Side Hustle – Days 25, 37

T

Tithing – Days 11, 68

Taxes – Day 36

Temptation – Days 19, 22, 39, 44, 64

Trusting God – Days 1, 4, 5, 12, 41, 43, 45, 86, 99

W

Work Ethic – Days 21, 24, 28, 31, 37, 40, 55, 83

www.ingramcontent.com/pod-product-compliance
Lightning Source LLC
Chambersburg PA
CBHW021241090426
42740CB00006B/633